# Pip's Puppies
## by Leonie Bennett

**Editorial consultant: Mitch Cronick**

# CONTENTS

Words in **bold** are explained in the glossary.

# My dog Pip

This is my dog Pip.

She is three years old.

Pip is a **golden retriever**.

Pip has got a fat tummy.

**Fat tummy**

# Going to the vet

The **vet** checks that Pip is well.

He feels Pip's tummy.

Pip is going to have puppies.

**Vet**

7

# Wow – my dog's a mummy!

We make a bed for Pip.

We put it in a quiet place.

Pip's bed

Blanket

The puppies are born.

One, two, three, four, five, six...

# Ten puppies!

There are ten puppies in the **litter**.

The puppies drink **milk** from Pip.

Pip licks them clean.

Then they go to sleep.

# Look at the new puppies

The puppies are two days old.

They can't see.

They can't walk.

They sleep a lot.

The puppies sleep together to keep warm.

# Watching the puppies grow

Now the puppies are four weeks old.

They can see.

They can walk.

The puppies sleep in a big box.

They want to get out
of the box!

# Time for dinner

Now the puppies are eight weeks old.

They can eat solid food.

They still like to drink milk from Pip.

This puppy is the biggest.

He eats a lot.

# Playful puppies

The puppies like to play.

They like to chew.

The puppies make puddles on the floor.

Sometimes they go to sleep in funny places.

# Saying goodbye

Now the puppies are ten weeks old.

This puppy is going
to a new home.

His new owner gives him a cuddle.

The puppy will ride in this basket.

21

# Glossary

**golden retriever**
A breed (type) of dog with a golden coat.

**litter**
The group of puppies all born at the same time.

**milk**
The drink produced by a mother to feed her puppies.

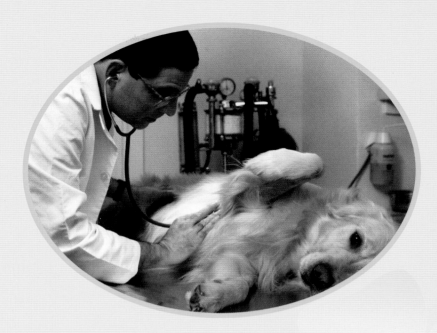

**vet**
An animal doctor.

# Index

Copyright © ticktock Entertainment Ltd 2008
First published in Great Britain in 2008 by ticktock Media Ltd.,
Unit 2, Orchard Business Centre, North Farm Road, Tunbridge Wells, Kent TN2 3XF
ISBN 978 1 84898 038 9 pbk
Printed in China

**We would like to thank: Shirley Bickler, Suzanne Baker and the National Literacy Trust.**

Picture credits (t=top, b=bottom, c=centre, l-left, r=right, OFC= outside front cover)
Colin Seddon photographer (Kaspurgold puppies): 12-13, 20. Corbis: 4. Kaspurgold Golden Retrievers (Phil and Susan Hocking): 2, 5, 10, 14, 15, 16, 17, 18, 19, 21. Shoonahs Golden Retrievers (Marilyn Barford): 1, 8, 9, 11. Superstock: 6-7.

**With thanks to all the dogs and puppies featured in this book – and their owners!**

Every effort has been made to trace the copyright holders, and we apologise in advance for any unintentional omissions. We would be pleased to insert the appropriate acknowledgements in any subsequent edition of this publication.